GET THE
BUSINESS

THE *Ultimate* BUSINESS GUIDE FOR ENTREPRENEURS

Build Your Business Profile and
Get Approved for Business Credit

ARNITA
JOHNSON-HALL

Get the Business: The Ultimate Business Guide for Entrepreneurs

Copyright © 2018 by Arnita Johnson

ISBN 978-1726291927

———————

To the business owner with great ideas but not enough capital to finance them, I've been where you are—an entrepreneur with high hopes and dreams of becoming successful and having a business you could be proud of. These were the expectations I had for my business when I first started. But there was just one thing holding me back...FUNDING!

WHAT'S INSIDE

HOW I GOT STARTED

S tarting a business is not easy and not having the capital to fund your business doesn't make it any better. This was pretty much my story 11 years ago when I was trying to get my business off the ground. I didn't have any startup capital, funding, or an inheritance.

Like most business owners and entrepreneurs, I started with what I had, which was roughly $200 at the time. I had always heard about business credit, but I honestly thought that the only business owners who could get approved were already successful in their business. In addition to that, even if I did get approved for business credit, I feared that I would put myself in more debt and wouldn't be able to pay my business debts if my company didn't grow or turn a profit.

So, I did what most entrepreneurs and business owners do when they start a business: USE PERSONAL ASSETS. My credit wasn't that great, but I had a few credit cards that had credit limits of about $2,000. I began to use my personal credit to fund my business. My personal credit suffered dearly because I began to max out my credit cards to purchase supplies and operate my business. Due to maxing out my credit cards, I attempted to apply for more credit cards and, of course, not only did I get denied, but I began to collect harsh inquires on my credit report due to my credit being ran so many times by lenders.

Several maxed-out credit cards, numerous inquiries, and a 100-point credit score decrease later, I decided to apply for business credit. What did I have to lose?

After much surfing the internet and studying, I realized that business credit wasn't just for large businesses. In fact, business credit was for any business that qualified for it. Lenders and vendors actually welcomed a business they could grow with. Besides, the more your business makes, the more money the lender makes. It's a win-win.

I was so excited to apply what I had learned, and soon after, I began applying for business credit. But I found myself discouraged and disappointed due to being continuously turned down and denied. I didn't understand it. Why was my business being turned down? What was I doing wrong? That's when it dawned on me. I was so busy applying for business credit just because I had a business name that I didn't take the time to establish and strengthen my business profile.

I'm sure you have experienced this too. There is always talk about how to "apply" for business credit but what information is out there telling us how to "establish" a business profile so you can get APPROVED for business credit?!

That was the missing piece to the puzzle. Once I began to establish and strengthen my business profile, I found it much easier for my business to get APPROVED for business credit. Once I was able to get business credit, I was able to fund and grow my business with the capital I received from lenders and vendors, and I no longer had to lean on my personal credit. I was also able to focus on growing my business instead of worrying about funding it.

Soon after I started to get approved for business credit, I began to build good relationships with several banks who specialized in assisting small business owners and entrepreneurs in getting business financing. I was surprised to learn that most of the business banking affiliates I had relationships with told me about banks and programs that are willing to loan small businesses the money to start or grow their businesses, however, they're unable to because these business owners have yet to establish their business profiles.

This information confirmed my thoughts and my own experiences. It wasn't the lack of business credit that was keeping small businesses from getting business funding. It was the lack of a strong and structured business profile. To date, my business has good credit scores, a good business report, and good business relationships with lenders and vendors. This is all with the help of establishing a strong business profile.

And this is why I created the *Get the Business* system. The *Get the Business* system is an easy step-by-step process to assist entrepreneurs with creating and strengthening their business profile to increase their business's chance of getting approved for business credit.

The *Get the Business* system is designed to take the headache out of applying for business credit blindly and to help your business look legitimate in the face of lenders. Everything I am telling you to do in this guide I personally did for my business, and it worked. This system has not only helped me establish my business profile so I could get approved for business credit, it has also helped hundreds of other entrepreneurs create business profiles for their businesses as well, and they were able to apply for business credit and get approved with ease.

I look forward to hearing the good news of your success.

But before we get started...

I have to be very honest with you. If your business already has a strong established business profile, then this guide may not be a good fit for you. This guide is not about how to get business credit. I recommend this guide to business owners and/or aspiring business owners who are looking to build and strengthen their business profile so they can get approved for business credit.

WHAT IS BUSINESS CREDIT

AND WHY IS IT SO DARN IMPORTANT?

Simply put, business credit is credit that is obtained in the name of a business. In addition, lenders will base the business's ability to pay back the loan based off the business's profile and the information inside of the business's credit report.

It is also important to know that your personal credit will not reflect or merge with your business credit UNLESS you are a personal guarantee. A personal guarantee is a business owner or business executive who legally promises to repay any debts in the event the business is unable to pay. This basically means the business owner or executive will be co-signing the loan with the sacrifice of his or her personal credit and/or assets. Not all lenders will require you to co-sign when applying for business credit, however, it is extremely important to make sure you have good credit and that you take care of it.

"Business credit is important because it helps you to not rely on your personal assets to go into business."

There are several reasons why business credit is important, and I am sure the answer will be different depending on the business owner you ask. In my opinion, business credit is important because it helps you to not rely on your personal assets to go into business. It also allows your business the opportunity to expand, build more capital and the cash necessary for your business to survive if managed properly.

HERE'S A LITTLE BUSINESS ADVICE

THE DO'S AND DON'TS

- Do follow the directions in this guide step-by-step.

- Do NOT jump the gun. Establishing your business profile will take time. This process can't be rushed.

- Do NOT apply for business credit if you do not intend to use it for your business.

- Do have a plan in mind for your business before you begin to apply for business credit.

- Don't overdo it! Applying for business credit can get addictive, especially if you're getting approved.

- Don't overextend your business credit. Overextending your business credit means you will be overextending debt.

- Do take care of your personal credit. There may be a time where you may have to co-sign for your business.

"" ""

Complacency can kill a company's profits. Oftentimes traditional methods become outdated. Even if you're the industry leader you should constantly seek new ways of doing things and evolving.

Keith Wilson

CEO of ClankIt

ARE
YOU IN
COMPLIANCE?

Below is the 20-requirement overview of what most banks and lenders will require before extending your business credit.

OVERVIEW

- **State Records:** *Your entity must be open, active, and in good standing.*

- **Federal EIN:** *Your Employer Identification Number filing must match your state filing exactly.*

- **Bank Account:** *The day you open your "business" bank account is the day your business starts in the eyes of lenders.*

- **Business Licenses:** *All applicable business licenses must be filed.*

- **DBA:** *Any "doing business as" must be on all state/ federal/banking records.*

- **Separate Business Phone:** *Your business must have its own phone number.*

- **411 National Directory:** *Business phone number must be listed with 411 under the exact legal name.*

- **Experian:** *File must be open with a credit history and good score.*

- **Dun & Bradstreet:** *File must be open with a credit history and good score.*

- **Equifax:** *File must be open with a credit history and good score.*

- *Business Credit Histories: No late payments or derogatory information on the business reports.*

- *Physical Address: The business needs its own physical address.*

- *Bank Rating: Your business bank rating should be at minimum a low five.*

- *Tax Returns: All applicable business tax returns must be filed.*

- *Public Records: There can be no liens, judgments or liens pending against the business.*

- *Credit Cards: At least three business credit cards with payments made early.*

- *Vendor Credit: At least five vendor lines of credit with payments made early.*

- *Comparable Credit: A larger loan from a nonbank lender with payments made early.*

- *Bank Loan: Securing a small bank business loan with payments made early.*

- *Business Model: A summary of your business plan with revenue projections.*

Even if you are already incorporated or have been in business for a while, it's crucial to make sure your business meets lender compliance so it can progress through the business credit building process.

Please keep in mind that these 20 items are just an overview of what you will be accomplishing in the *Get the Business* system. You do not have to start working on anything yet. I will be addressing each of these items in the coming steps.

Now that you know what we are going to do, let's get the business!

CHECKPOINT SYSTEM

Check off all the requirements you already have. This will allow you to stay organized and on track. No sweat if you do not have all the requirements. Remember, this is NOT a race.

My goal is to have this completed by:

_____ / _____ / _____

☐ State Records: Your entity must be open, active and in good standing.

☐ Federal EIN: Your Employer Identification Number filing must match your state filing exactly.

☐ Bank Account: The day you open your "business" bank account is the day your business starts in the eyes of lenders.

☐ Business Licenses: All applicable business licenses must be filed.

☐ DBA: Any "doing business as" must be on all state/federal/ banking records.

☐ Separate Business Phone: Your business must have its own phone number.

☐ 411 National Directory: Business phone number must be listed with 411 under the exact legal name.

☐ Experian: File must be open with a credit history and good score.

☐ Dun & Bradstreet: File must be open with a credit history and good score.

☐ Equifax: File must be open with a credit history and good score.

☐ Business Credit Histories: No late payments or derogatory information on the business reports.

☐ Physical Address: The business needs its own physical address.

☐ Bank Rating: Your business bank rating should be at minimum a low five.

☐ Tax Returns: All applicable business tax returns must be filed.

☐ Public Records: There can be no liens, judgments or liens pending against the business.

☐ Credit Cards: At least three business credit cards with payments made early.

☐ Vendor Credit: At least five vendor lines of credit with payments made early.

☐ Comparable Credit: A larger loan from a nonbank lender with payments made early.

☐ Bank Loan: Securing a small bank business loan with payments made early.

☐ Business Model: A summary of your business plan with revenue projections.

THE "BIG" THREE

BUSINESS CREDIT BUREAUS

Business Credit Bureaus also known as business credit reporting agencies are for-profit companies who collect data from banks, suppliers, vendors, credit card issuers, finance companies, and public records such as tax liens, bankruptcies, and judgments and compiles the information in a business credit report. The business credit bureau will also report your business's credit history and will use such information to calculate your business credit score. Lenders will then determine your business's creditworthiness based on this information.

Although there are tons of business credit bureaus out there, there are three that reign high and mighty. Those three business credit business are Experian Business, Equifax Small Business, and Dun & Bradstreet.

EXPERIAN

EQUIFAX

DUN & BRADSTREET

WHO IS EXPERIAN BUSINESS?

Experian Business is one of the dominant players in the industry with over 27 million companies listed in its database. One major difference is it does not allow you to self-report trade references like Dun & Bradstreet. The only way to get listed is by doing business with a creditor or supplier that furnishes data to this specific agency.

WHO IS EQUIFAX SMALL BUSINESS?

Equifax Small Business is another agency that plays a significant role in the industry with over 80 million companies listed in its database world-wide. This agency is said to be one of the most difficult to get listed with and most of its data reporters are banks and leasing companies. Similar to Experian Business, the only way to get listed is through a creditor, lender, or business that supplies its payment data to Equifax Small Business.

WHO IS DUN & BRADSTREET?

Dun & Bradstreet is the world's leading source of commercial information with over 237.7 million companies listed in its database and over 1.5 million updates per day. Many suppliers, lenders, and leasing companies share and pull business credit reports from Dun & Bradstreet to assess the credit worthiness of businesses.

The D-U-N-S° Number is recognized, recommended, and/or required by more than 200 global, industry, and trade associations, including the U.N., European Commission, and the U.S. Federal Government.

"

Most people think they need an investor to start a business without realizing they already have one: their job! Use your paycheck to fund your business until your business is profitable enough to fund you!

Courtney Sanders

Think and Grow Chick

THE IMPORTANCE OF A BUSINESS NAME SEARCH

t is important to do a name search on your business name for three reasons. For one, you want to make sure your business name does not conflict with anyone else's. Next, you want to ensure your business name does not cause any trademark or copyright infringements. Lastly, you want to make sure your business name is not taken by anyone else. Trust me, there's nothing far worse than having a business name, falling in love with it, and finding out that it already belongs to someone else. Or perhaps there's nothing worse than filing a business name and finding out that it conflicts with someone else and being sued for it.

It's also important to make sure your name is unique to further ensure your business won't get confused or mixed up with any other business, especially when filing for business credit. You don't want to apply for business credit and constantly have to explain why your business name is NOT the same as the business name you're always getting mixed up with.

CONDUCTING A BUSINESS NAME SEARCH

Conduct a business name search by following these steps:

STEP 1

Do a company name search with Dun & Bradstreet to see if any businesses with the same or very similar names are listed with Dun and Bradstreet (D&B). To use D&B's company name search, visit http://www.dnb.com.

STEP 2

Checking a national name search registry to ensure your business name does not conflict with other businesses (or is already taken) can be a little tricky. The reason is because there are so many public databases and name search registries out there. I recommend doing several name searches with the following companies/agencies:

1. Secretary of State
2. County Clerk's Office
3. USPTO
4. Network Solutions
5. The Thomas Register

STEP 3

Make sure your business is not committing "Trademark Infringement." Trademark Infringement is the unauthorized use of a trademark or service mark (or even a similar mark) on competing or related goods and services. In much easier terms, "doing business as" or using a business name that is the exact same or is similar to a competing company's name.

To conduct a Trademark Infringement name search, check with the U.S. Trademark office. This search is absolutely free. Visit the USPTO website at http://www.uspto.gov/trademark. From there, click on "Trademark Search" and select "Basic Word Mark Search (New User)" to submit a query.

STEP 4

Perform a domain search/website address search. The reason why it is important to do a domain search or website address search is to make sure your website address for your business name is not currently being used. To do that, you can visit any domain hosting site like Godaddy.com or Hostgator.com. You should purchase your business name URL (domain name) if it is available as a ".com." For example, if your business's legal name is "The Auto Store," then "www.TheAutoStore.com" needs to be available and you should secure it. It's also vital to purchase the .net, .co, and .org domain extensions to your .com URL to ensure no one tries to take it.

STEP 5

Web Listing/Online Directory Search. You'll need to search the online directories to see if your business is listed correctly or even listed at all. If your business shows up, make sure all of the information is correct. If it does not show up, be sure to create a free business listing with the Superpages Directory and Express update (InfoGroup).

CHECKPOINT SYSTEM

The business name search will be completed by:

_____ / _____ / _____

☐ Dun & Bradstreet

☐ National Name Search Check

☐ Trademark Name Search

☐ Domain Name Search

☐ Web Listing/Online Directory Search

TAKE NOTE

_____

_____

_____

_____

_____

"

Your purpose is what's really going to pay you. Spend time discovering what you are called to do so that you can finally start living the life of your dreams.

Koereyelle DuBose

CEO of WPS Media Group

BUSINESS CREDIT

FOUNDATION BUILDING

Building a solid business foundation to strengthen your business profile is vital. When applying for vendor credit, business credit cards, cell phone services, and especially a bank loan—LENDERS WILL DO THEIR RESEARCH!

Any little thing that doesn't match or add up may get your business flat-out denied! Remember, this is nothing like establishing personal credit. Putting all of this together will take time. I have separated these steps into lessons. I recommend reading all of the lessons, then go back and complete the action steps.

> *"Any little thing that doesn't match or add up may get your business flat-out denied."*

LESSON 1

YOUR BUSINESS SHOULD BE AN ENTITY

Action items for this step:

☐ Set up a business entity or make sure your business entity is set up correctly.

☐ File Foreign Corporation if required (See Special Note on the next page for more details).

Strengthening your business profile to get approved for financing is also about paying attention to details. It is very important that you use your exact business legal name. This includes the recorded DBA filing you will be using. It is not required to have a DBA, but if you need one (or already have one), there are potential issues to be aware of.

"Doing business as a separate legal entity is the only way to completely separate your personal credit from your business's credit."

Filing DBAs for your Corporation or LLC can cause multiple credit files to open if you're not careful. For example, say your business bank account is under "ABC Corporation" but you open a credit account as "ABC Corporation DBA "ABC Tire Service," and you have another credit account that you opened as just "ABC Tire Service."

What will happen in the above example is that your business ends up with three open credit files under all three names, and now you have a mess. If you're going to use a DBA, you'll need to avoid creating duplicate credit files. All banking, utilities, office leases, credit accounts, etc., must be opened as "ABC Corporation DBA ABC Tire Service."

Why Do You Need a Business Entity to Build Business Credit?

It is best to build business credit with an LLC or Corporation (S or C Corporation). Creditors, lenders, trade accounts and other vendors prefer to see an actual business entity. Furthermore, filing and using a business entity to build business credit can separate you personally from the liability of operating your business. Unless you're required to operate as a LLP or other type of partnership (medical practice, law firm, CPA, etc.), you should create a business entity. Your personal and business credit can never be truly separated if you operate as a sole proprietorship or partnership—everything you do remains "personal."

Form a Corporation or LLC

In order to maximize your "fundability" and build a business credit profile that is separate from your personal credit, you need to form a type of corporation or LLC. If you need to form a separate entity, I recommend Legal Zoom. It's easy, quick, and the reps are always helpful and nice. Once you've formed a separate entity for your business, you must make sure everything relating to the business is done in the business's name.

SPECIAL NOTE

If the state where your business was formed does not match the state of its primary location, then your business will need to file for "Foreign Corporation" status in the state where it is located and does business. For example, if your business was incorporated in Nevada or Delaware but its primary location is in California or New York, then you will have to file for Foreign Corporation status in either California or New York.

TAKE NOTE

TAKE NOTE

TAKE NOTE

_____

_____

_____

_____

_____

_____

_____

_____

_____

_____

_____

_____

_____

_____

_____

_____

_____

_____

_____

_____

TAKE NOTE

" "

If you're too cute to start from the bottom, you're obviously too cute to get this money.

Raevyn Jones

Busy Being a Millionaire

LESSON 2

OBTAINING A BUSINESS ADDRESS FOR YOUR BUSINESS

Action item for this step:

☐ Get a business address for
your business.

Business Address & Location

The address of your business
needs to look like a business
address. Do NOT use a post
office box. You can use your
home address for business
credit building but be aware
that some lenders will not fund
home-based businesses. This
will not stop you from building
business credit scores but may
limit your funding options.

> *"Your business address is an important component. You can have a home-based business, but it may limit your access to certain lenders."*

Obtaining a True Business Address

To properly establish and build credit, your business needs a de-
liverable physical address and not a PO Box. In fact, many lenders
and credit providers may flag your business even if you try to use a
reformatted address from service locations like the UPS Store, USPS
Mailboxes, and Postal Annex, etc.

If you don't have an actual storefront or office location, you can run
your business from anywhere and still have a qualifying business
address with solutions like these:

1. **Address Only** - Receive mail and packages at your dedicated
   business address.
2. **Virtual Office** - Professional business address with dedicated
   phone and fax numbers, receptionist services, and part-time

use of fully-furnished offices and meeting rooms.

3. **True Office** - Your own full-time private office with receptionist services, dedicated phone and fax, internet, full furnishings, meeting rooms, and more.

TAKE NOTE

_____

_____

_____

_____

_____

_____

_____

_____

_____

_____

_____

_____

_____

TAKE NOTE

TAKE NOTE

TAKE NOTE

TAKE NOTE

"

No matter how small, treat your business like a corporation and everyone else will have no choice but to respect it as one.

Arnita Johnson-Hall

LESSON 3

BUSINESS PHONE, 411 NATIONAL DIRECTORY LISTING AND FAX

Action items for this step:

☐ Ensure that the business has a dedicated business phone number.

☐ Ensure that the business has a dedicated business fax number.

☐ Submit your business phone number to the 411 National Directory.

☐ Verify that your business phone number is properly listed under 411.

"You need a business phone number that is listed with 411 National Directory Assistance. And your business needs a fax number even if it's a virtual one."

The perception lenders, vendors, and creditors have of your business is critical to your ability to build a strong business profile. This perception is why I highly recommend you have a business phone number listed under 411, a dedicated fax number, and even an 800 number. These items are important components of building your business profile and boosting the perception of your business.

1. Business Phone Number

You must have a dedicated business phone number that is listed with 411 National Directory Assistance under the business name. Do NOT use your home number. Lenders, vendors, creditors, and even insurance providers will verify that your business is listed with 411. A toll-free number will give your business credibility, but you must have a LOCAL business number for the listing with 411 National Directory Assistance.

Boost Perception with an 800 Number

How do lenders, vendors and customers see you? It's just too easy and inexpensive to add a virtual toll-free 800 or 8** number as one of your business numbers. Even if you're a single owner with a home-based business, a toll-free number provides the perception that you are a real business. Some of the advanced features include: multiple extensions, customizable music (e.g. for placing on-hold), voicemail, flexible call-forwarding options, and more. Plans for toll-free numbers or even virtual numbers for your local area code start as low as $9.95/ month with most companies.

Whether you're applying for financing with a lender or net credit terms with a vendor, providing a cell or home phone number as your main business line could get you "flagged" as an unestablished business that is too high of a risk. I do NOT recommend giving a personal cell phone or residential phone as the business phone number.

2. Business Fax Number

Many people say that faxing is a thing of the past. That is simply not true when it comes to lenders and credit providers. As a business, you will need a fax number to receive important documents and to fax credit applications.

Virtual Fax

There are many great services where you do not need a fax machine and all of your faxes are accomplished via the internet. Interested? I recommend Ringcentral.com or Grasshopper.com.

If you set up a virtual office solution, it will include a dedicated fax number.

3. Business Phone Number

To get your business phone number listed, contact your local phone carrier. Keep in mind that you'll need to have your phone service with them in order to get a number listed.

A third option is to list your business with ListYourself.net. The service is free and has been proven to be very effective to solve the 411 National Directory Assistance listing. On the website under the "businesses" tab, complete the form. Once the form is submitted, you will need to verify that you are listed under 411. To do this, you will dial your area code followed by 555-1212 and then simply ask for the listing of your exact business legal name. If possible, do not use a cell phone to check your listing.

In addition, since searching the internet is the number one tool used to locate a business today, it's crucial to make sure your business is listed on major online business directories. While there are many popular online directories to get listed with, there are several key sites that play a role in the business credit-building process.

Certain online directories are the online equivalent of a modern-day phonebook, so getting listed is a great way for not only customers to find you but also lenders to verify your business listing in the 411. Here are the top online business directories to submit your business listing with:

Facebook for Business
http://www.facebook.com/

To create a business page for your business on Facebook, you will need to have a personal account. Click on your name in the upper right-hand corner and scroll to the bottom. From there you will see a selection for "Create a Page." Fill out all the information that is asked thoroughly. Make sure you update this page regularly and add a link to it from all your online websites. It will take some time and is a slow process. Don't be discouraged at first if you only receive one new like per month. It will slowly grow into being an excellent resource to efficiently spread timely news and events about your business, and best of all, it's free.

Yelp!
http://www.yelp.com/

You will need to create an account. Be sure to check your inbox to verify your email address before you try to add your business. Search for your business's name in the upper search bar and the zip code where your business is located. When the page loads, it should tell you that there were no matches found and give you the option to add a business. This website allows your customers to leave reviews on your business which is definitely an asset.

Yahoo!
http://local.yahoo.com/

At the bottom of the page, you will see a link to "Add a Business." Once you select that, it will ask you to sign in. If you already have login credentials for Yahoo!, sign in or you can create an account. It takes approximately four to five days for final approval before you will see your business listed.

Yellow Pages (YP.com)
http://www.yellowpages.com/listing_feedback/new

Take a moment to check their site just to make sure you aren't already listed. The link above will take you directly to the form for listing your business.

Super Media
http://www.supermedia.com/spportal/quickbpflow.do

You can follow the steps on this site to see if your business is already listed and even add, update, or change information about your business.

Yellowbook
http://www.yellowbook360.com/internet-yellow-pages

You will need to click on the "Request a Consultation" to have a representative contact you regarding your listing. Yellowbook no longer offers the ability to complete these steps online, however, their support staff is excellent and will assist you with all your needs.

Manta
http://www.manta.com/

It's as easy as scrolling down to the middle of the page and clicking "Get Started." Then, follow the instructions. You will have to pick up the phone and call Manta to confirm your listing and that you are an actual person. At the very end of the process, you will see a choice of different programs that you can purchase. Just know that even though it appears you have to pay for the listing, once you call in with the verification code, there is a link in the middle of the page to say, "No thanks."

Google+ for Business (Formally Google Places)
http://www.google.com/+/business/

Google search "Google Places Business." Once you find the right page, it will ask you to sign-in with your Google login (the same for your personal Google+ account which accesses your business account). Google Places will ask for your business phone number and guide you through the rest of the process. To verify your information, if they do not already have your business listed at your address, they will send a postcard in the mail with a verification code for you to fill out your information.

Bing Business Portal
http://www.bing.com/businessportal/

Select the option on the left that does not require log-in information. Bing will then give you the option to search for your business. If there is already a listing, you can claim it, and if not, you can create a new one. You will need to provide contact information and communication preferences. Bing gives you a lot of details to fill out—even a QR code and mobile website are created for you. Be sure to list as much information as possible. The more you provide, the better the chances that your customers will find you. You will have to verify your business if it is a new business. You can select to have a letter sent to you with a PIN number which will take approximately seven to 10 days.

Local.com
http://www.local.com/

You should see a link in the middle of the page that says "List Your Business for Free." Be sure to type your entry quickly when you are doing your business listing. It timed-out on me twice while I attempted to enter business details. You can definitely add details to your listing without upgrading to a premium listing. It looks a little confusing, but just continue inputting details until it goes through.

Merchant Circle
http://www.merchantcircle.com/

Select "Join Now." Have your set of keywords available to include with your listing and be prepared to verify your listing through your email. Merchant Circle gives you a lot of great features to update your listing. Be sure to go into your listing's control panel when you finish the first set of questions to add additional details and your business logo. You can also select a member name to make your URL unique and easier to get to. You also have the ability to add an owner image (I have found that if you include an actual headshot, potential customers connect better with your business).

Each listing that you create online takes time and it is best to thoroughly complete each one so you will not have to go back to each one. The most useful part of filling out each one is that these sites have a much higher search engine ranking than you could ever hope to have starting out. It's all about exposure when your potential customers are searching online. The more listings you have with the most detailed information the better chances you will be found.

It is necessary for you to take the time to list all of these as accurately and completely as possible. Find a place to store this information so you do not lose it, and can keep track of all the places that you have listed your information.

TAKE NOTE

TAKE NOTE

TAKE NOTE

TAKE NOTE

" "

The money is already printed,
you just got to go get it.

Jackie Nicole

Boss Chicks

LESSON 4

BUSINESS WEBSITE AND PROFESSIONAL EMAIL ADDRESS

When credit providers research your company on the internet, it is best if they learned everything directly from your company's website.

Many business owners fail to see that not having a company website is hurting their chances of obtaining multiple trade lines from various vendors. There are many places online that offer affordable business websites, so you can at least have an internet presence that displays an overview of your company's services and contact information.

"Having a business website with your corporate email address is no longer just a good business idea. Credit providers are now looking at this."

Action item for this step:

☐ Obtain a business email address via a hosting service.

Don't Overlook the Need For a "Professional" Business Email Address

It is important to get a company email address for your business. It's not only professional but greatly helps your chances of getting the thumbs up from a credit provider. A great example is an email like support@yourcompany.com or johnsmith@yourcompany.com. Avoid using free services like Yahoo and Hotmail.

The email address must be "@yourcompany.com." There is nothing worse than potential credit providers noticing your company email address is partychic2009@yahoo.com. Setting up a business email address is just too easy and inexpensive to neglect.

Basic Business Website and Professional Email Address

Lenders and credit providers will check to see that you have both a professional website and email address. Whether you want a new website that is custom built for your business or you'd like your existing website upgraded or "remodeled," there is a solution.

Go to GoDaddy's® website: www.godaddy.com. Use this site to check the availability of your domain name. If your business name is already taken as a ".com" address, try some variations of it like .net or .org. You can also try variations of the business name itself until you find an available one, then buy it. Here are some domain extensions to explore:

- .com
- .org
- .net
- .mobi
- .info
- .us
- .biz
- .tv
- .ws
- .eu

TAKE NOTE

TAKE NOTE

TAKE NOTE

TAKE NOTE

LESSON 5

FEDERAL EIN & BUSINESS LICENSES: CITY, COUNTY, STATE

Action items for this step:

☐ Obtain EIN

☐ Obtain business license

Whether you have employees or not, your business entity must have a Federal Tax ID number (EIN). Just like you have a social security number, your business has an EIN. Your Tax ID number is used to open your bank account and to build your business credit profile. If you have an EIN, you may still need a new one if:

> *"You need an Employer Identification Number (EIN) to use as your business credit identity. You also need the proper licensing from your city, county, or state."*

1. Your business is subject to a bankruptcy proceeding.
2. You form a new corporation or change the corporate name.
3. You take in new partners and operate as a partnership.
4. You purchase or inherit and plan to operate an existing business.

Please take the time to verify that all agencies, banks, and trade credit vendors have your business listed with the same Tax ID number. To obtain an EIN or to determine if you need a new one, call the IRS directly at 800-829-4933 or simply have a professional service provider do it for you.

Business Licenses

One of the most common mistakes when building credit for your company is to have business addresses on your business licenses that do not match. Even worse is not having the required licenses for your type of business to operate legally. You will need to contact the state, county, and city government offices to see if there are any required licenses and permits to operate your type of business. You can contact them directly via phone or search their websites to confirm if there are any required licenses or permits for your type of business.

Example:
You start up a business and operate it out of your house. In this instance, some cities might require you to have a license while other cities may not.

TAKE NOTE

TAKE NOTE

TAKE NOTE

TAKE NOTE

TAKE NOTE

LESSON 6

BUSINESS BANK ACCOUNT IS WHEN YOU STARTED

Action item for this step:

☐ Get a business account

Decide which bank you want to open an account with, then call or email them. Ask what their specific requirements are for opening a business checking account. Generally, most banks require a copy of your business certificate from the secretary of state, an IRS document with your EIN on it, and sometimes your articles of incorporation. The date you open your business bank account is the day lender's consider your business to have started. So if you incorporated your business 10 years ago but you just opened the business bank account yesterday, then your business started yesterday.

> *"Your business bank account must be opened under the exact state and federal filing name. And the day it opens is the day your business started."*

Banking Name

The first step in establishing a strong business profile is with bank credit. Make sure your business name and mailing address listed on your business bank account(s) matches exactly how your business name and address appear on your legal paperwork that has been filed with the state. It must also match exactly with the name and address that appears on any Federal EIN paperwork. If it does not match, GET IT CORRECTED IMMEDIATELY.

Banking History

Most lenders will not determine the age of your business by the date that appears on your Incorporation, LLC, or EIN paperwork. The date you filed paperwork is of no concern to lenders or to the business credit agencies. Everything in business lending and business credit starts from the day you open your business bank account.

Your business banking history is vital to your future success of being able to secure larger business loans. Lenders will look to see how long that relationship has been established. The longer your business banking history, the better your borrowing potential.

Merchant Credit Card Processing

Most businesses can benefit from being able to accept credit cards as payment for their products and services. Could your business benefit? There is no shortage of sources out there that can provide you with a merchant account, a processing gateway, and any necessary equipment so you can accept credit cards from your customers. In fact, your bank will more than likely want to be that merchant solution for your business.

However, it's important to explore your options before setting up a merchant account with your bank. It might be convenient but can also greatly limit your financing and credit options both short-term and long-term. For example, there are funding programs based on your merchant processing and not on standard credit underwriting that can provide ongoing access to cash for your business.

TAKE NOTE

TAKE NOTE

TAKE NOTE

TAKE NOTE

LESSON 7

ALL AGENCY LISTINGS MUST BE EXACTLY THE SAME

Action item for this step:

☐ Make sure all your business names are reporting the correct information and that it all matches.

"Every agency and creditor must list your business the exact same way. Now is the time to audit everyone you're listed with to ensure consistency."

You must confirm that every agency, creditor, supplier, and trade credit vendor has your business listed the exact same way. You must be listed with the exact same spelling of your business name and the exact same address and phone number.

For example, one might have you listed as "ABC, Inc.," while another has you as "AB Consultants;" and yet another as "AB Consultants, Inc.." There are also simple differences like those between "Suite 400," "#400," and "Apt. 400." The differences are important, and they should be corrected where possible.

Take the time to verify that these main agencies (state, IRS, bank, and 411 National Directory) have your business listed the same way and with your exact legal name. Also take the time to ensure every bill you get (power bill, phone bill, landlord, etc.) has the business name listed correctly and comes to the business address.

This is very important: Pay attention to detail and MAKE SURE YOU DO IT NOW!

The following agencies are vital to your business financing and business credit building success:

1. Your state
2. Your county
3. Your city
4. Your bank
5. The IRS
6. 411 National Directory Assistance

TAKE NOTE

TAKE NOTE

TAKE NOTE

TAKE NOTE

TAKE NOTE

CHECKPOINT SYSTEM

- [ ] Your currently available funding programs

- [ ] State business filings listed correctly

- [ ] County license and/or permit filings listed correctly

- [ ] City license and/or permit filings listed correctly

- [ ] IRS filings listed correctly

- [ ] Bank account listed correctly

- [ ] 411 National Directory Assistance listed correctly

TAKE NOTE

_____

_____

_____

_____

_____

_____

_____

BONUS: OBTAIN A D-U-N-S NUMBER

N ow you need to go to Dun & Bradstreet and obtain a D-U-N-S Number. In two or more years of building business credit, I have noted one ever constant factor—Dun & Bradstreet. It is the leading cause of headaches for businesses trying to build a credit file. New business owners are especially prone to the sales pitches thrown by commission-hungry DUNS sales reps. Just about every new business owner tends to ask a question about DUNS or ends up complaining about them.

The front lines of D&B are covered by the DUNS sales representatives. More often than not, if you are trying to get a DUNS number from them, it starts the vicious cycle of how worthless simply having the number will be and how you "need" to buy CreditBuilder or another product to have a full-rated file. The plain and simple fact is, you do NOT need to buy anything from DUNS to end up with a fully-rated file! DUNS sales reps will, of course, try and tell you otherwise in hopes of making you pay.

Unlike personal credit CRAs, DUNS is not governed by the FCRA. They are a loose canon existing within a realm of pure gray area when it comes to regulation. Simply put, they can screw you and get away with it if you're not careful. First thing that has often been misunderstood is that you need to get a DUNS number in order to have a file. Or that you need to contact DUNS to open a file or get a number. This is misinformation.

A DUNS number can and is automatically created by one of the following:

a. When your first NET30 account reports the trade line, the DUNS system will automatically create your number and file.
b. If you are incorporated, the Secretary of State in your state will often automatically report your corporation's existence as it reports quarterly or semi-annually to DUNS.

I am unsure if every states' SOS office in fact does this, but many I know do. The best bet for auto-creation is to simply open some starter NET30 Internet-based office suppliers (see below). Be sure and use the account and then promptly pay the invoice. Most of these places will open you a NET30 terms account with as little as a 411 phone listing for your company. There are enough of these vendors out there to use if one or the other gives you grief, insisting they need to see a credit file. Some of these vendors may ask you to place an initial pre-paid order. No biggie. Get it out of the way and move on to having a NET30 terms account. Many will open you one from the start—no questions asked.

If you need a DUNS number immediately, it can often be obtained from the government contracts site:

http://fedgov.dnb.com/webform/pages/CCRSearch.jsp

It's just as easy to let it auto-create, though. The thing is you MUST be PATIENT! It's not going to all happen in a day or even a week. If you miss out on the vendors reporting cycle, it may take a number of weeks for the NET30 to report. But given your alternative route of calling the main DUNS numbers and getting grief from the commission-hungry reps, and possibly getting your file flagged by a rep who is going to try to hamstring you or otherwise extort services from you, it would be wise to just let it auto-create.

Again, you DO NOT need to call DUNS to get a number or file. Just like Experian Business files, DUNS will auto-create with the SOS or first trade line data. When you do a search on DUNS for your business and it finally shows up, then you want to get eupdate access. In order to access your eupdate report, you need two things: your DUNS number and a eupdate password. The easiest way to accomplish this is to click your business when it shows up in a search. It will give you several different types of reports you can buy for your company. Select the cheap $9.99 basic report. All you want is the DUNS number. Buying more expensive reports will not likely yield any additional info given how new your company is. Don't waste your money. Spend the $9.99 and buy the report. You will then get to see your DUNS number.

OK, now go to eupdate at https://eupdate.dnb.com/ (Keep in mind that the eupdate site is frequently down for whatever reason.)

Bookmark this page. But do not do anything yet because chances are if you fill out the sign-up info at this point, you're just going to get an error page saying your entered info doesn't match what's on file. The real problem actually is that your report doesn't have all the info on file for the eupdate system to match against. Instead, call the entity department at 1-866-834-4699. Tell them your DUNS number and that you are having an issue getting your eupdate password. They will either verify company info with you right then and there, or they will take your company and phone number and put you on the callback list for their department. If they tell you the rep will call you, they will, and be sure to answer the phone when you see them calling (this department is not the sales department). They will run down the company info asking about biz stats and owners, etc. They will probably ask for financials to round out your report. All this really means is they want a copy of a balance sheet. If you don't do them typically, go on Google and find a balance sheet template and fill it out. They will give you a fax number to send it to.

After they take your info, you need to let the new info register into their system. This may take a day or two. At this point, if they haven't already emailed you an eupdate password, the info that will allow the system to send you one should now be on their system and you can go up to the aforementioned eupdate link and sign up. They should simply send you one within a day or two after taking all your info.

When you talk to the rep at the above number or the one that calls you back, be sure to get their direct number and extension to follow up should they put an error in your file like an incorrectly spelled name or phone number. When you get your eupdate password, log in. Do not choose the edit profile option. Just choose the one that lets you see the report. Any time you hit the edit button, DUNS keeps a running count and if you go into edit mode too much, they will flag your file. You can get updates done easier when dealing with this department. Most things you enter into eupdate will get you a verification call from DUNS anyway, so just don't screw with the edit section.

Also don't look at your eupdate every day. Updates are typically only done once a week and visible on Sundays, so look on Sundays.

OTHER HELPFUL HINTS

- *Do NOT go on application sprees. Inquiries set off alarms with DUNS and gets your file sent to an early fraud department which often results in your file being frozen with all reporting data and ratings removed.*

- *There is NO reason to call the main DUNS numbers or even deal with the sales team. There is not even any good reason to go get your DUNS number as apposed to simply letting it auto-create. I know some folks need it for government bidding, but plan it out ahead of time and get the number by auto-creation, and you will have taken a serious step at avoiding the frontline sales people that is the main reason for most people's complaints.*

- *There are departments within DUNS who are not on commission and will never try to sell you a thing.*

ABOUT ARNITA

Arnita Johnson-Hall, CEO and Founder of AMB Credit Consultants, educates consumers on how to restore, obtain, and maintain good credit. With her 11+ years of business experience, extensive expertise of credit education, and burning desire to help like-minded entrepreneurs build attractive business profiles that get them approved, Arnita has a life mission to empower business professionals with the knowledge and resources they need to live and maintain a life of financial stability.

Made in the USA
Middletown, DE
14 January 2021

31528595R00062